Prehistoric Beasts UNCOVERED

Tyrannosaurus rex
King of the Dinosaurs

By Dougal Dixon

RUby TUesday BOOKS

Published in 2018 by Ruby Tuesday Books Ltd.

Copyright © 2018 Ruby Tuesday Books Ltd.

Editors: Ruth Owen and Mark Sachner
Designer: Emma Randall
Production: John Lingham

Photo Credits:
Alamy: 6 (bottom), 8, 9 (top), 12 (top), 14 (top), 15, 27 (bottom); Dr. Antoine Bercovici: 25 (bottom right); Black Hills Institute of Geological Research, Larry Shaffer (2004): 12 (bottom); Burke Museum: 24 (top) Larry Mose, 24 (bottom) Dave Demar, 25 (top) Dave Demar, 26 top, 27 (top); David A. Burnham, University of Kansas: 18 (top); Tom Connell: 21, 22—23; Kieran Davis: 25 (bottom left); Gregory M. Erickson, Ph.D.: 28 (top); Aaron Fredlund: 18 (bottom); Getty Images: 9 (bottom left), 20 (bottom), 28 (bottom); James Kuether: 10, 19; Public Domain: 9 (bottom right), 11 (bottom), 17 (centre), 19 (top), 28 (centre); Ruby Tuesday Books: 17 (bottom); Science Photo Library: 14 (bottom); Shutterstock: Cover, 2, 4—5, 6—7, 11 (top), 13, 20, 26 (bottom), 29, 31; Franco Tempesta: 16, 17 (top).

British Library Cataloguing In Publication Data (CIP) is available for this title.

ISBN: 978-1-911341-75-8

Printed in Poland by L&C Printing Group

www.rubytuesdaybooks.com

Contents

Naming the King

All living things have a **Latin** scientific name in two parts – a **genus** name and a **species** name. You are *Homo sapiens*. A dog is *Canis familiaris*. It is the same with dinosaurs – *Triceratops prorsus*, *Stegosaurus stenops* and, of course, *Tyrannosaurus rex*. When a scientific name is abbreviated it should be written like this: *T. rex*.

What Does **Tyrannosaurus rex** Mean?

tyrannos = tyrant   *sauros* = lizard   *rex* = king

It's a hot, steamy evening on the island continent of Laramidia. Insects buzz around tall redwood trees. A herd of hadrosaurs is grazing low-growing flowers with their broad, duck-like beaks.

But in this peaceful scene, a deadly threat lurks.

A fearsome predator waits in the leafy shade.

Its nostrils take in the scent of the prey.

Its enormous teeth become coated
with saliva in anticipation.

The unsuspecting hadrosaur herd
comes closer,
and closer . . .

King of the Dinosaurs

With a crash, the great animal charges from its hiding place. It is a huge male *Tyrannosaurus rex* — the biggest and most powerful meat-eater on the continent. There is no escape for one of the hadrosaur herd.

A Deadly Attack

As the hadrosaurs wheel and turn in panic, one female, smaller and younger than the rest, is unsure what to do. Her moment of hesitation is fatal. The great jaws of the hunter crash down on her neck, stripping flesh, shearing **tendons** and crushing bone. She is dead in seconds, and crumples at her attacker's feet.

Is this how *T. rex* captured its prey?

Predator or Scavenger?

Was *T. rex* a solitary **ambush** predator, lying in wait for unsuspecting plant-eaters to come along? Or did *T. rex* hunt in packs as lions do today? Maybe *T. rex* was mainly a **scavenger**, eating the remains of animals that were already dead? What can **fossils** and other types of prehistoric **evidence** tell us about *T. rex*? Can we uncover the secret world of the King of the Dinosaurs?

Teeth Like Knives

Two types of lethal, banana-shaped teeth lined *T. rex*'s great jaws. At the front were thick, stubby teeth for grabbing and holding on to struggling victims. At the sides of the jaws were teeth with flattened edges. These teeth were serrated, like a saw or steak knife. They were designed for slicing meat off the bones of its prey.

A fossilised *T. rex* tooth

Serrated edge

20 cm

How Big Was *T. rex*?

The largest and most complete skeleton found to date is a *T. rex* nicknamed Sue.

Length: Up to 12.8 metres

Height at hips: 3.66 metres

Estimated weight: 8400 to 14000 kilograms (the weight of two African elephants)

Meet T. rex

We all think we know what *Tyrannosaurus rex* looked like, don't we? The problem is that our idea of what it really looked like has changed over the last 100 years as more and more information has come to light. And it is changing still.

Building a King

For 80 years, we thought that *T. rex* stood upright. In 1915, the first *T. rex* skeleton to be shown in this way went on display at the American Museum of Natural History (AMNH) in New York City.

Three fingers on each hand

A long tail dragging on the ground

T. rex on display in 1915

Two Claws

The three fingers on the hands of the 1915 skeleton were from a different dinosaur altogether. Then other tyrannosaurs were found to have hands with only two fingers. In 1989 a complete *T. rex* hand was found that proved *T. rex* had two clawed fingers on each hand.

Rebuilding the King

By the 1980s, dozens of *T. rex* skeletons had been found. Scientists also knew that birds **evolved** from dinosaurs. A bird stands with its feet directly beneath its hips. Scientists realised that the balance of *T. rex*'s whole body was at the hips, a little like a seesaw. The heavy head and body could be held forward because they were balanced by the big tail. In 1994, the AMNH skeleton was remounted.

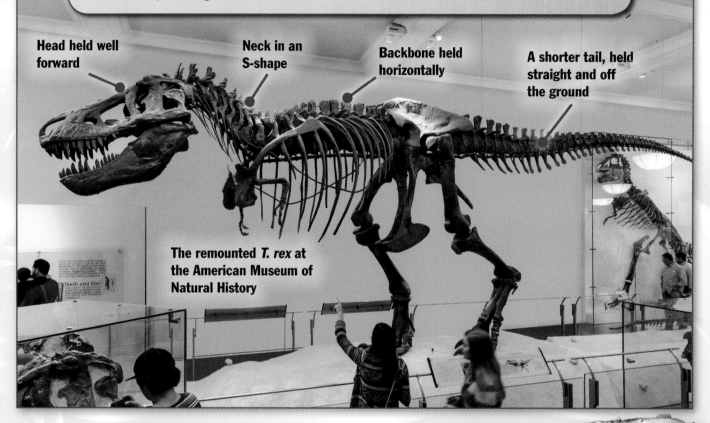

Head held well forward

Neck in an S-shape

Backbone held horizontally

A shorter tail, held straight and off the ground

The remounted *T. rex* at the American Museum of Natural History

Tail

Tail muscle

A *T. rex*'s arm could lift about 200 kilograms – the weight of two large adult men!

Mr Muscle

Scientists can work out the shape of *T. rex*'s muscles by looking at "muscle scars". These are marks on bones where muscles were attached. Muscle scars show that *T. rex*'s tail carried a massive muscle that was attached to the top of its legs. This muscle powered the animal's walking. *T. rex*'s arms were also very strongly muscled despite their tiny size.

T. rex's World

Tyrannosaurus rex lived in western North America at the end of the **Cretaceous period**, around 66 million years ago.

Meet the Family

Before *T. rex* became king of the continent, Laramidia was home to other tyrannosaurs. These early relatives of *T. rex* evolved on the land mass that we now call Asia. In time, they crossed over a land bridge into Laramidia. By 70 million years ago, Laramidia was home to several large meat-eaters.

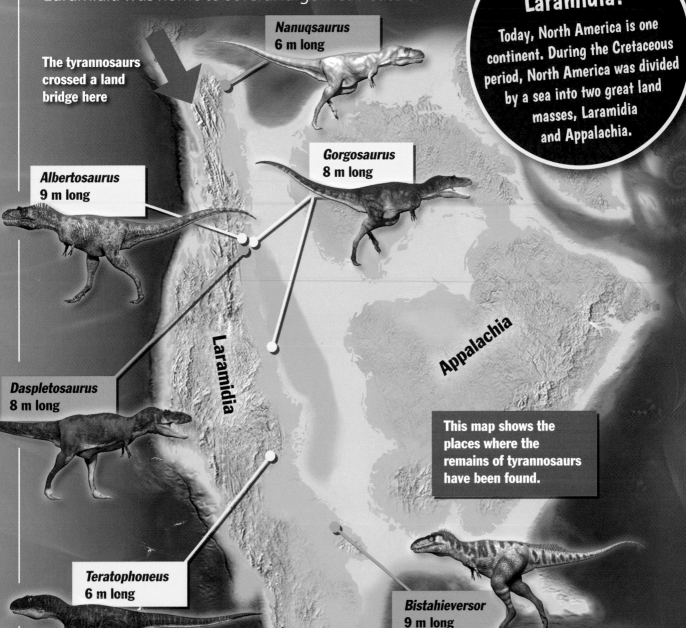

Where Was Laramidia?

Today, North America is one continent. During the Cretaceous period, North America was divided by a sea into two great land masses, Laramidia and Appalachia.

Nanuqsaurus
6 m long

The tyrannosaurs crossed a land bridge here

Gorgosaurus
8 m long

Albertosaurus
9 m long

Laramidia

Appalachia

Daspletosaurus
8 m long

This map shows the places where the remains of tyrannosaurs have been found.

Teratophoneus
6 m long

Bistahieversor
9 m long

T. rex Becomes King

T. rex was the last tyrannosaur. It lived at the very end of the Age of Dinosaurs. *T. rex* may have evolved from an animal like *Daspletosaurus* that was already in Laramidia. Another **theory** is that it evolved from its close relative *Tarbosaurus* in Asia and then migrated to North America.

The Last Tyrannosaur

One thing we do know is that by the late Cretaceous period no other tyrannosaurs existed in North America. *T. rex*'s relatives had all become extinct. *T. rex* was the continent's biggest and most powerful predator.

The land where *T. rex* lived was steamy and swampy.

This is the area known as the Badlands in Montana. Many *T. rex* fossils have been found here.

The Land of *T. rex*

Many *T. rex* fossils have been found among the hot, dry cliffs and mountains of the Hell Creek Formation in the Badlands of Montana, USA. When *T. rex* lived here this area looked very different. The land was covered with forests and swamps, and the climate was warm and wet, like today's rainforests.

Scales or Feathers?

We know *Tyrannosaurus rex*'s size and shape from its fossilised bones. But what did *T. rex* actually look like? For many years, scientists believed that *T. rex* had **scales** like today's reptiles. However, there was no evidence to prove or disprove this theory.

Meet the Feathered Family

In 2004, a dog-sized tyrannosaur named *Dilong* was discovered. This tiny relative of *T. rex* had a body covered with feathers. In 2012, a larger feathered tyrannosaur, named *Yutyrannus*, was also discovered. These fossil finds led scientists to rethink their ideas. Was it possible that *T. rex* had feathers like its relatives?

A model of a feathered *Yutyrannus*

The largest *Yutyrannus* skeleton that's been found is 9 metres long.

Prehistoric Skin

In 2017, a team of scientists made an exciting announcement. They had found patches of fossilised scaly skin on the skeleton of an adult *T. rex*. The skin was from the animal's neck, chest, stomach, pelvis and tail.

Fossilised scales from a *T. rex* that was found in Montana, USA.

What Do We Know?

The discovery of fossilised scaly skin proves that *T. rex* definitely had scales on some parts of its body. But did *T. rex* have feathers or bristles on other places, such as its back? Maybe. Until more evidence is found, no one can say for sure. . . .

Perhaps *T. rex* had a cloak-like covering of feathers or bristles along its spine.

The King of Cool

Scientists think there's a good reason why *T. rex*'s whole body wasn't feathered. *T. rex* was an enormous animal. When walking or running, its giant body would quickly overheat. Not having a full covering of feathers made it easier for *T. rex* to stay cool.

What Colour Was *T. rex*?

For now, we don't know what colour *T. rex* was. We can only make guesses based on the colours that work for modern animals. Perhaps *T. rex* was grey or brown. Big animals, like elephants and rhinos, are usually a dull colour all over their bodies. If *T. rex* attacked its prey by ambush, it may have hidden itself with **camouflage**, like today's tigers and leopards.

A *T. rex* with camouflage markings for hiding in forests and swamps.

13

Get Inside T. rex's Head

Most dinosaurs are only known from one **specimen**. Sometimes, just a single bone has been found! When it comes to T. rex, we are very lucky. Over many years of searching and digging, scientists have found 15 T. rex skulls.

Scanning a Dinosaur's Skull

Even though an organ such as a brain cannot survive millions of years, we know the shape and size of T. rex's brain. How? Scientists can use a **computed tomography (CT) scanner** to look inside a dinosaur's skull. A CT scanner is a special kind of X-ray machine that is usually used in hospitals to see inside patients.

T. rex's brain case

A computer model of a T. rex's brain

This large area controlled T. rex's sense of smell.

T. rex's Brain

Inside a T. rex skull there is an empty space called the brain case. This area once contained the animal's brain. By scanning the skull and brain case, scientists can build a 3D computer image that shows the shape of T. rex's brain. By comparing the different parts of the brain to the brains of modern animals, scientists can find out information about T. rex's senses.

The largest T.rex skulls measure up to 1.45 metres long.

Hunter Vision

T. rex had eyes that faced partly forwards. This would have enabled it to see in 3D and judge distances – just as a cat does when pouncing on prey. This ability, along with its flexible neck, allowed *T. rex* to spot, follow and catch fast-moving prey. The shape of *T. rex*'s eyes show its vision was possibly as good as that of a modern-day eagle.

A Nose for Scavenging?

The shape of *T. rex*'s brain shows scientists that it had a good sense of smell. This sense would be essential for a scavenger that fed on **carrion**.

Listening for Prey

The part of *T. rex*'s brain that dealt with hearing shows it could hear very low sounds – for example the noise made by footsteps. This kind of hearing would have helped *T. rex* find distant prey.

A Sensitive Snout

Scientists have studied a well-preserved skull of a dinosaur called *Daspletosaurus*. This dinosaur was a close relative of *T. rex*. On its jawbones they discovered tiny pits, or holes, that contained **sensory nerves**. Modern-day crocodiles have similar nerves which give them very sensitive snouts. From this evidence, scientists think that *T. rex* probably had a highly sensitive snout, too. This would have been helpful when looking after fragile eggs. Perhaps a *T. rex* even rubbed faces with its mate!

A T. rex Grows Up

Wouldn't it be great if we found fossils of *Tyrannosaurus rex* eggs and babies? Then we could discover more about the family life of this huge predator.

The Search for a Baby *T. rex*

About 50 *T. rex* skeletons, in various stages of growth, have been found. But no one has ever found a very, very young one. The youngest *T. rex* skeleton discovered was about the size of a labrador. The animal was probably about two years old when it died.

A T. rex Nest

Scientists have discovered fossil eggs and nests of other meat-eating dinosaurs. These finds show us that the eggs were hard shelled, like birds' eggs, not soft like crocodile eggs. Like birds, female dinosaurs sat on their eggs to keep them warm until the babies hatched. We can only guess that it was the same for a mother *T. rex*.

A baby *T. rex* hatches from its egg

A Young *T. rex*'s Life

A young *T. rex* was a different shape from a grown-up. It had a narrow snout with more teeth than an adult. It also had longer legs, with lightweight feet and lots of muscle on the thighs. These are the legs of a fast-running animal that probably hunted small, quick-moving prey. It's likely that a young *T. rex* was covered with feathers.

Narrow snout

Long legs

Scientists think this skeleton is a juvenile *T. rex* that was about 11 years old. It is 6.5 metres long.

Growing Up Fast

Dinosaur bones have growth rings like the ones we find in tree trunks. From these rings scientists can see that a young *T. rex* grew slowly at first. Then it put on a great growth spurt between the ages of 14 and 18, when it became an adult. From the skeletons found so far, scientists think *T. rex* probably lived for about 30 years.

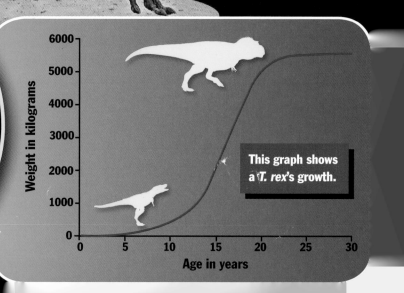

This graph shows a *T. rex*'s growth.

A Meal Fit for a King

Was *Tyrannosaurus rex* a hunter or a scavenger? It was possibly both. Like today's big cats, *T. rex* could hunt live prey. But if it found a dead body, it would take advantage of a free meal.

T. rex the Hunter

In South Dakota, USA, scientists found a fossilised hadrosaur tail bone, with a broken-off *T. rex* tooth stuck in it. New bone had grown around the tooth. This shows the hadrosaur was still alive when *T. rex* attacked, and it must have escaped and survived.

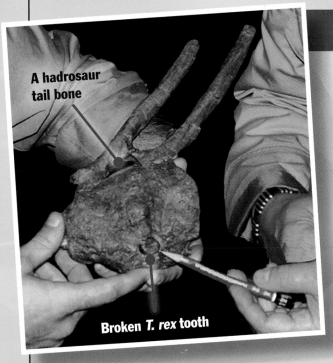

A hadrosaur tail bone

Broken *T. rex* tooth

T. rex the Scavenger?

In Montana, USA, a *Triceratops* skeleton was found that had been torn to pieces by a hungry *T. rex*. It looks as if the flesh was pulled off by the small teeth at the front of the snout. The bones had been crushed by the big teeth on the sides of the jaws. Scientists cannot tell, however, if the *T. rex* killed the *Triceratops*, or found the corpse already dead.

A tyrannosaur print from the fossil trackway

T. rex the Pack Hunter?

We don't know yet if *T. rex* lived and hunted alone or in a pack. It's possible, however, that other tyrannosaurs which came just before *T. rex* lived in groups. In 2011, a fossil trackway was discovered in British Columbia, Canada. It shows three adult tyrannosaurs walking in the same direction at the same time. The tracks may have been made by *T. rex*'s relatives *Albertosaurus*, *Gorgosaurus* or *Daspletosaurus*.

Dino Dung

Fossilised lumps of *T. rex* dung, called **coprolites**, contain undigested fragments of hadrosaur bones. The coprolites show that *T. rex*'s digestive system was like a crocodile's. Food passed quickly through the system, leaving the bones only partly broken down by stomach **acids**.

Some *T. rex* coprolites are about 50 cm long!

Piece of undigested bone

A *T. rex* attacking a type of hadrosaur called *Edmontosaurus*

T. rex would have swallowed bone as well as flesh to get calcium.

Illness, Injury and Death

All living things suffer accidents or become ill at some time. Often, this leaves some sort of mark on a skeleton.

Bones Tell a Story

Specimens of elderly *T. rex* often have backbones fused together. This can happen when new bone grows to repair damage after a fight. *T. rex* even suffered from a painful bone disease called gout, caused by its diet of red meat.

Like modern-day animals, *T. rex* probably fought over food and mates.

T. rex Had Spots!

Some *T. rex* skulls have deep holes in the jaws. In life these would have appeared on the skin as large pus-filled spots in and around the mouth. The spots were caused by an infection that still affects modern birds. The holes may even be from tooth marks that became infected after a fight with another *T. rex*.

are a sign of

The King Is Dead!

Once a *T. rex* died, its body may have rotted in the sun, been washed away in floods, or eaten by scavengers. This is why it's very rare to find a complete fossil dinosaur. There is usually nothing left to fossilise!

Studying Dinosaurs

By studying the marks on fossilised bones, a scientist can tell something about the way a dinosaur lived. This study is called pathology. Some scientists study how living things became fossils. This is called taphonomy.

At the end of its life, a *T. rex* lies down and dies by the side of a stream.

Insects gather to lay their eggs on the carcass.

Belly becomes bloated by gases.

Days pass and the carcass begins to decay. The flesh dries out and shrivels in the sun.

Scavenging animals, such as crocodiles and pterosaurs, eat the rotting flesh.

Big meat-eaters, including other *T. rex*, eat and carry off whole bones and large parts of the carcass.

The rainy season comes, and the remains of the *T. rex* are covered by floodwater.

Bones are washed here and there. Some are washed away completely. The skeleton becomes less and less complete. . . .

T. rex Becomes a Fossil

The Bones Are Buried

The *Tyrannosaurus rex*'s bones are covered by a layer of mud and sand deposited by the floodwaters.

65 Million Years Ago

The stream becomes a river that deposits sand and mud on top of the skeleton. Over tens of thousands of years, more and more layers of **sediment** build up on top of the bones.

The bones that remain move no further. Above the skeleton, the floodwaters become a stream.

A sea forms, flooding the area. **Groundwater** penetrates the bones. The structure of the bones starts to change as they turn to **mineral**.

Over millions of years the layers of sediment are crushed and cemented together, forming limestone rock.

30 Million Years Ago

More and more layers of rock form. Movements in the Earth's crust push the rock upward. High above the skeleton, mountains form. The rocks are twisted and torn by the movements.

The skeleton has become a fossil inside the rock. It is broken and twisted as the rock moves.

2 Million Years Ago

The mountains stop moving and growing. Wind, rain and snow begin to wear them down.

As thousands of years pass by, the T. rex skeleton moves closer and closer to the surface.

Today

As the rocks around it are worn away, the fossilised skeleton begins to appear.

One day, the tip of a bone is found by accident.

Excavating *T. rex*

Once a skeleton is found it has to be **excavated** as quickly as possible. This is to stop it being destroyed by the weather and **erosion**.

Uncovering a Skeleton

In 2015, the bones of a large carnivore were discovered in the Hell Creek Formation, in Montana. In 2016, a team from the Burke Museum in Seattle, USA, began an excavation at the site. The **palaeontologists** soon discovered the skeleton belonged to a *T. rex*!

The Bones Are Revealed

The overburden, or layer of rock above a skeleton, is removed by diggers, or by people using large drills, axes and shovels. Next, the team uses brushes, trowels and chisels to uncover the bones. Photographs are taken of the skeleton and a map is drawn of the bones before they are moved.

Overburden

Palaeontologists

T. rex's rib

A team of around 45 people worked at the dig site for two summers.

The Burke Museum's palaeontologists cover the *T. rex*'s skull with plaster.

A Protective Jacket

A skeleton must be transported to a **laboratory** for careful study. The sections of the skeleton, still in the surrounding rock, are encased in a protective plaster jacket. The jacket is similar to a plaster cast used by a doctor to fix a broken bone.

Encased in its plaster jacket, the skull weighed 1360 kilograms.

On the Move

Heavy vehicles, such as trucks and tractors, are needed to move the sections of a large skeleton. Farmers, local businesses and the army sometimes donate vehicles. Even helicopters may be used to lift a skeleton.

The Tufts-Love Rex

The *T. rex* that was uncovered in 2016 has been named the Tufts-Love Rex after Luke Tufts and Jason Love, who discovered the bones. From the size of its skull, scientists estimate it was about 15 years old when it died.

Tiny Clues

Scientists study samples of the rock from around a skeleton. This can give them a fuller picture of the time when *T. rex* was alive.

Fossilised crocodile teeth found amongst a *T. rex*'s bones show that crocodiles fed on the carcass before it was buried.

This image shows fossilised Cretaceous pollen seen through a microscope. Pollen can tell us what kind of plants covered the land where *T. rex* lived.

Into the Laboratory

Clinging to the side of a dusty, windy cliff is not the best place to study the remains of a *Tyrannosaurus rex*! So once a skeleton is excavated, it is taken to a safe, clean laboratory.

Preparing a Fossil

At a laboratory, specialist technicians, called preparators, remove any rock and carefully clean up the fossil bones. This work takes skill, patience and many months. Finally, the fossils are ready for the scientists to study.

Fossil skull

Matrix

Plaster Jacket

Jaw

Teeth

Removing the Matrix
Fossil bones arrive at a laboratory still embedded in the matrix, or rock. Chisels, dental tools and brushes are used to remove the rock.

Preparators at the Burke Museum slowly revealed the skull of the *T. rex*.

Into the Acid
Sometimes, if the matrix consists of limestone, preparators put the specimen in a bath of acid. The acid eats away at the limestone and can leave the fossil quite clean. This process can take many months.

Dental tools

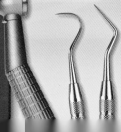

Sand-blasting tool

Cleaning It Up

Any remaining rock is delicately removed from a fossil by blasting fine sand on to the specimen with a high-pressure stream of air. This is done with a pen-like piece of equipment that allows the preparator to have control over the process.

Fossil bone has a dark, shiny, cracked surface.

Looking Inside a Bone

It's not usually possible to tell the sex of a *T. rex* from its skeleton. But in 2016, a scientist named Mary Schweitzer announced she had discovered one piece of evidence. Female birds produce a special kind of bone called medullary bone. This bone acts as a store for calcium, which the bird uses to build eggshells. Mary found medullary bone in the thigh bone of an adult *T. rex*. This proved the animal was a female, and she was about to lay eggs.

From Bone to Stone

A fossil bone has spent millions of years under immense pressure deep within rocks. It has undergone chemical changes brought about by heat and groundwater. The living tissue has fossilised and become a mineral. Fresh bone is white, chalky and very light. Fossil bone is dark, shiny and heavy as stone – that's because it has become stone!

A fossil *T. rex* foot

T. rex the Bone Crusher

Once a *Tyrannosaurus rex* skeleton is in a laboratory and prepared for study, all kinds of scientific techniques can be used to learn more about the animal.

Measuring Bite Force

How powerful was *T. rex*'s bite? That was the question that scientists Greg Erickson and Paul Gignac wanted to answer. To find out, they measured the bite forces generated by the jaws of alligators and crocodiles. Then they compared the modern animals' jaw muscles to *T. rex*'s jaw muscles.

Greg Erickson measures an alligator's bite force.

A computer model of *T. rex*'s tooth pressure.

Top teeth

The bone cracks under pressure

Bottom teeth

T. rex's Jaws

Muscle scars on a *T. rex*'s skull show where its jaw muscles were attached. By measuring the scars, it's possible to calculate the size of the muscles.

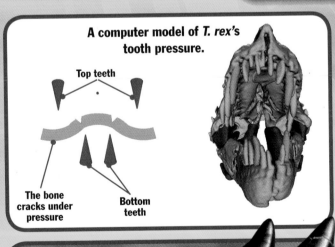

T. rex had the largest teeth of any dinosaur that ever lived.

The Result: Exploding Bones!

The data showed that *T. rex*'s jaws could generate about 3600 kilograms of force. Its bite was like the weight of three cars pressing down onto its victim. The scientists also studied *T. rex*'s teeth. The size and positions of the biggest teeth allowed *T. rex* to produce bone-shattering pressure. If *T. rex* were alive today, its bite force and tooth pressure would enable it to crush and rip up a car!

Did *T. rex* Roar?

Fearsome animals today make fearsome noises. Lions and tigers roar, wolves howl — but what noises did fierce, predatory dinosaurs make?

Did *T. rex* Sound Like an Ostrich?

Big cats and wolves are mammals. Like other mammals, they have voice mechanisms in their throats and they release their sounds through open mouths.

Dinosaurs were more closely related to birds and would not have possessed the same noise-making structures. It's more likely that dinosaurs made deep, booming sounds, like modern ostriches and emus. The sounds would have travelled for long distances along the ground.

Like an ostrich or emu *T. rex* possibly made sounds with its mouth closed.

The Sound of *T. rex*

To understand how *T. rex* might have sounded, scientist Julia Clark tried to recreate its voice. Using a mixing desk, she combined the booming sound of a bird called a bittern with the low, growling rumble of a crocodile. Then she adjusted the sound so it matched the size of a *T. rex*. Julia created a deep, sinister *whumpf*, *whumpf* noise. Is this how *T. rex* sounded? No one can say for sure!

Glossary

acid
A substance, usually a liquid, that has the ability to attack and break down certain other substances.

ambush
Attacking unexpectedly from a hidden position.

camouflage
Colours, markings, coverings or body parts that help an animal blend into its habitat.

carrion
The rotting flesh of a dead animal.

computed tomography (CT) scanner
A machine that takes a series of highly detailed, cross-section photographs of a person or animal's body.

coprolite
Fossilised animal dung. Coprolites are useful to palaeontologists — they tell what a fossil animal had been eating and how it digested its food.

Cretaceous period
A period in time that came between the Jurassic period and the Paleogene period. It lasted from 145.5 million years ago to 66 million years ago. The Cretaceous period was the end of the Age of Dinosaurs.

erosion
The process by which a rock or a landscape becomes worn away. Weather, rivers, landslides and even walking animals all cause erosion.

evidence
Information that can be used to show that something is true. For example, the shape of *T. rex*'s fossil teeth are evidence that it was a meat-eater.

evolve
To change or develop slowly, often over a long period of time.

excavate
To dig into the ground to uncover something, such as a fossil.

fossil
The hard remains of a living thing that are preserved in rock.

genus
A classification of living things. A genus may cover several species. For example, the genus *Panthera* has several species, including *Panthera leo*, the lion, and *P. tigris*, the tiger.

groundwater
Water that has soaked into the ground and collected in the soil or between rocks.

laboratory
A room or building where there is equipment that can be used to carry out experiments and other scientific studies.

Latin
A language that began in ancient Rome. Scientists still use Latin today when naming animals, plants and other living things.

mineral
A solid material that is formed by natural processes and is found in soil or water. Rocks are made of minerals.

palaeontologist
A scientist who studies animals and plants from the past.

scales
Thin, tough, flat plates, or sections, of skin that form the covering of an animal.

scavenger
An animal that feeds on carcasses or dead plants.

sediment
Particles of sand or mud that have accumulated at the bottom of a river, lake or ocean.

sensory nerves
In an animal's body, the network that carries signals to the brain.

species
Different types of living things. The members of an animal species look alike and can produce young together.

specimen
A sample of something used for scientific study.

tendon
The springy material that attaches an animal's muscles to its bones.

theory
An idea or belief that is based on limited information. A theory can be proved with evidence.

Index

Learn More Online
Could you be a scientist uncovering the buried secrets of prehistoric beasts?
Go to: www.rubytuesdaybooks.com/dinosaurs